Existentialism and Humanism

This lecture was delivered by Jean-Paul Sartre in Paris in 1945; it is a defence of Existentialism as a doctrine true to Humanism, and is followed by a discussion which shows how well Sartre could hold his own against criticism.

Jean-Paul Sartre was awarded the Nobel Prize for Literature in 1969. He died in Paris in 1980.

Existentialism and Humanism

JEAN-PAUL SARTRE

Translation and Introduction by
PHILIP MAIRET

Methuen

The French edition of this book was published in 1946 by Les Editions Nagel, Paris, under the title *L'Existentialisme est un humanisme*

First published in Great Britain by Methuen & Co. Ltd in 1948
First paperback edition published in 1973
New paperback edition published in 2007

Reprinted 2008, 2009, 2010, 2011, 2013, 2014, 2015, 2016, 2017, 2018, 2019, 2020, 2021, 2023, 2024, 2025

Methuen
www.methuen.co.uk

Copyright © Editions Gallimard, 1996

Translation and Introduction © Methuen & Co. Ltd, 2007

Without limiting the author's, translator's and publisher's exclusive rights, any unauthorised use of this publication to train generative artificial intelligence (AI) technologies is expressly prohibited. Methuen Publishing Limited also exercise their rights under Article 4(3) of the Digital Single Market Directive 2019/790 and expressly reserve this publication from the text and data mining exception.

The rights of the copyright holders have been asserted in accordance with the Copyrights, Designs and Patents Act, 1988

ISBN: 978-0-413-77639-6

A CIP catalogue record for this book is available from the British Library

Printed and bound by CPI Group (UK) Ltd, Croydon, CR0 4YY

This book is sold subject to the condition that it shall not, by way of trade or otherwise, be lent, resold, hired out or otherwise circulated without the permission of the publishers in any form of binding or cover other than that in which it is published and without a similar condition, including this condition, being imposed on the subsequent purchaser.

Registered office: 1 Wheelgate, Malton, YO17 7HT

CONTENTS

Note   vii

Introduction   1

EXISTENTIALISM AND HUMANISM   23

Discussion   69

NOTE

The occasion upon which the author developed the fundamental ideas published in this book was a lecture delivered at the Club Maintenant. He repeated it privately in order to give the opponents of his teaching the opportunity to state their objections. Their various interventions, and the author's replies to them, appear after the text of the lecture.

Introduction

Although the existential movement in France has had almost a popular success, it is much more than a passing fashion in ideas. It has over a century of history behind it, and is already entitled to rank as one of those movements of revolt against over-systematisation in philosophy which have occurred from time to time in the course of Western thought, with corrective or stimulating effect. And although existentialism is often described as anti-historical, and in a sense it is, its advocates show no lack of interest in their historical antecedents. The present translation of a lecture by Jean-Paul Sartre, followed by a discussion, may therefore be usefully prefaced by a brief account of the school of thought which it represents.

The first statement of the existential theme was made when the great age of German philosophy had culminated in the Hegelian system of dialectic. That imposing edifice of thought, which was to dominate the minds and disorder the affairs of generations to come, provoked a solitary Danish philosopher, Sören Kierkegaard, to vivid and voluminous contradiction. This remarkable man, to whom all existential thinkers acknowledge their indebtedness, led a life that was almost as uneventful externally as that of Oblomov, with an inward history that was even richer in emotional drama, and of a phenomenal intellectual activity. Never did a more troubled soul, or a more lucid and swift intelligence, seek enlightenment from the learned only to reject it as valueless. The case that he was continually arguing against the great systematisers, original as it was in presentation, sparkling with humour, illustration and anecdote, was not so new as it was profound. He saw that most philosophy is not even wisdom after the event, but only wisdom about wisdom and little to do with any event. Neither the Kantian analysis of mind nor the Hegelian evolution of thought and history was of any help when one came to the making of one of those individual human decisions upon which the real course of events depends—yes, and the development of thinking too. It is only minor decisions, upon which nothing of great importance hangs, that can proceed serenely from such detached deliberation: the genuine, critical dilemmas of the individual's life—and to

Kierkegaard individuals alone were real—are not solved by intellectual exploration of the facts nor of the laws of thinking about them. Their resolutions emerge through conflicts and tumults in the soul, anxieties, agonies, perilous adventures of faith into unknown territories. The reality of every one's existence proceeds thus from the "inwardness" of man, not from anything that the mind can codify, for objectified knowledge is always at one or more removes from the truth. "Truth," said Kierkegaard, "is subjectivity."

For it was in the subjective sphere, in the inward relation of oneself to oneself and to the subjectivity of others, that one became aware of God and of a relation to Him. The idea of God still dominated most of the speculative philosophy of the age of Enlightenment, though it was depersonalised as the Absolute; of such were the philosophies that ruled the academic teaching of Kierkegaard's time and place. The philosophers themselves were Christian, more often than not, some of them devoutly so. So were their contemporaries, the great scientists; but the philosophers' work, like theirs, did much to accelerate men's flight from the God of faith. By analysing Being into hierarchies of ideas and series of categories, they acted as the great secularisers of public

Introduction

thinking: they did, in a sense, objectify God as thought. What was omitted from this development of ideas was the real subject — man, in the total, unfathomable inwardness of his being. Looking back upon that period of thought in the light of its consequences, one can scarcely deny that the protest of Kierkegaard had at least the typical justification for a philosophic rebellion. He spoke up for what was being neglected or ignored.

The literary works of this great writer are, in consequence, more theological than philosophical in the usually accepted sense of the word, but Kierkegaard's talent for metaphysical discussion is undeniable. It is expressed mostly upon the critical side, however; his positive contributions lie in the sphere of aesthetics, ethics, and what may be called the psychology of the spirit. Distrusting all mysticism as much as he dislikes abstract philosophic theorising, Kierkegaard bases his position upon individual man here and now, man in his passion and anxiety; and much of his argument is founded openly upon personal experience, including that of the erotic crisis of his life which was, externally, of an ordinary, almost commonplace description. He writes of man as a being with a passion for happiness — for an eternal happiness — and if this would not actually have been his definition of man, it is the only kind of man Kierkegaard writes for, or expects to understand him. Three resolutions of the problem of passion are explored in his writings—the aesthetic, the ethical and the religious—sufficiently systematically to give form and unity to his work as a whole. The highly unorthodox method of Kierkegaard's writing—its emotional range, extending from utterances of the profoundest piety to a rather garrulous levity—probably did more than his substantial unorthodoxy, which is not easy to pin down, to prevent his wide acceptance as a religious writer. But a religious writer he is, first and last, and for all his rebellions against the Protestant church in which he was for a time a preacher, his ultimate purpose is the rediscovery and vindication of the traditional faith. As he says at the end of his *Final Postscript*, the motive that runs through all his writings is the desire "to read *solo* the original text of the individual human existence-relationship, the old text, well known, handed down from the fathers, to read it through yet once more, if possible, in a more heartfelt way."

And heartfelt is the word: even now, a hundred years after, Kierkegaard has an extraordinary power of establishing intimate personal contact with his reader, of making one feel that what one reads is addressed to one

Introduction

individually. In this, which is the best exemplification of his doctrine possible in letters, Kierkegaard is far and away the greatest as well as the first of existentialists. Yet at his death his works fell into extreme neglect. Except to a small extent in Germany, they remained practically unknown outside his native land until well into the present century; and the successive translation of all of them into English is a phenomenon only of the last ten years.

During the intellectual disorder between the two great wars, however, Kierkegaard's influence made itself strongly felt in Germany, and was associated with certain currents of post-Nietzschean thought. For Nietzsche, who seems never to have heard of Kierkegaard, was an existentialist in his almost romantic emphasis upon the passion, anxiety and decision of individual man, and had a similar sense of the tragic predicament of humanity in modern civilisation. The two thinkers are poles apart, of course; but that means that the world of ideas which their relative positions define is recognisably the same world. Even Nietzsche's fierce contradiction of Christianity, which is a negative statement of its vital bearing upon man's complete individuation, has points of relation to Kierkegaard's sublime anti-clericalism. Nietzsche's Superman and Kierkegaard's Knight of Faith are both conceptions of the transcendence of passion and intellectualism through the power of some purely inward integrity, though the one is an integrity of mastery and the other of obedience. These ideals are at least alike in the quality of their subjectivity.

The posthumous co-operation of two such different authors shows, however, the ambiguity in what is called existential doctrine. The more purely subjective the criteria by which values are estimated, the less clearly they can be applied to the judgement of real affairs such as cultural questions, political doctrines, social tendencies or the conclusions to be drawn from history. Whither, outside of the psychology of the spirit in its quite narrow and personal connotations, does existentialism lead? Hitherto, existential thought has branched in the two main directions of religious philosophy and of a secular activism that is still anti-religious. The most important of modern developments in Protestant theology, in which Barth and Brunner are the most illustrious names, is largely of existential origin. But so is the completely secular philosophy of Heidegger, and his work is the principal source of contemporary French existentialism. There are no signs, at present, that this ambiguity is likely to be resolved, or that the two main streams may not

Introduction

diverge still more widely, or branch into smaller rivulets and ultimately soak away in the sands of time. Even if they did, however, the challenge of existentialism to the religious, rationalistic and materialist philosophies of our time would not therefore have been fruitless. And in the immediate future, this movement of thought is much more likely to grow than disintegrate.

Philosophical variations can never be wholly explained by reference to surrounding social and historical conditions, important as these are to the full understanding of them, for ideas often spread across geographical boundaries and periods of time; they germinate anew wherever they find individuals with the mentality and sensibility favourable to their growth. But there can be no doubt that the social circumstances and the prevalent moods of defeated Germany—indeed of Central Europe generally—in the 1920's were fertile soil for this seed of subjective absolutism. Extreme disillusionment prevailed as to the political and social systems upon which men had previously relied, and their discredit extended to all the cults and systems of objective thinking that had been associated with them. In such circumstances men try to get back to the roots of their knowledge in search of a more secure basis of life. They are ready to question the authenticity of all the beliefs, principles and institutions they find around them, and much more willing than in better times to seek for the truth in subjective and psychological spheres.

The apprehension of environmental insecurity, and the searching analysis of its causes are very closely related to the existential motive in the writings of Karl Jaspers, a professor of philosophy at Heidelberg, one of the two leading minds in German existentialism. His *Man in the Modern Age* is mainly a powerful indictment of the progress of contemporary technological civilisation, which he regards as a social disease; ever-growing reliance upon objective criteria of thought having been paid for by ever-deepening ignorance of the real nature of human existence. No less tragically than Spengler, whose influence was at its height in Jaspers' early prime, he foresees a "decline of the west," and to Jaspers the fatality inherent in this culture is its effect upon the minds of individuals: the surrounding world grows so dense with objective and mechanistic systems of thought that the will is progressively stifled. The surrender of man's thinking to rationalism and of his artifice to technics have consequences which console man with the feeling that he is progressing, but make him neglect or

Introduction

deny fundamental forces of his inner life which are then turned into forces of destruction. "*The sclerosis of objectivity is the annihilation of existence.*" Jaspers' statement, that if the logic of technical progress should lead to the destruction of human existence on earth there would now be nothing to prevent it, seems more alarmingly probable today than when he wrote it. He is a professed Catholic, who sees no escape from the nemesis of our culture except in man's recognition that, although he can never be other than a free being, he can also never be self-sufficient; he is free to open his life—but in anguish—to the influence of the living God, or in pride to deny and repel Him. Thus Jaspers' argument culminates in a religious philosophy, one which is perhaps no more and no less assimilable to accepted Christian traditions than that of Kierkegaard. But whereas Kierkegaard's premonitions of the doom of mechanised Christendom are often startlingly accurate, they are intuitions that pierce through the prosperous appearances of early nineteenth century Europe to its nemesis in the future. The fate of Jaspers' world is already overtaking it, and the study of man's secular conditions occupies a great part of his work; much of his vindication of subjectivity is a demonstration of the secular consequences of its neglect.

But to Martin Heidegger, Jaspers' contemporary and a philosopher of Fribourg, there is nothing beyond man himself that can solve the problem of man's existence. Heidegger is a thinker of importance, whose permanent contribution to philosophy is considerable. He is also the existentialist who stands out most characteristically in the intellectual tumult of shell-shocked Europe, a man full of insights into all the psychological, psychoanalytic and speculative philosophies of his time, familiar with all their burrowings into the subconscious in search of a new philosopher's stone. Many interesting and important things these movements did bring to light, including the data of phenomenology; and Husserl, the chief exponent of phenomenology, was a teacher of Heidegger.

Phenomenology is a highly scientific branch of psychology, not, like psychoanalysis, concerned with the effective and emotive aspects of the mind, but based upon the study, largely experimental, of its perceptual faculties. An adequate description would be far beyond the scope of this introduction, but it may be useful to mention a very simple fact of phenomenological importance. If we draw, for example, a black maltese cross upon a white square, we can perceive either the cross itself, or the spaces between its limbs, as the statement that is

Introduction

being made, but we cannot perceive it both ways at once. In the latter case—taking the black as spaces between—we see the figure as a conventionalised four-petalled flower in white upon a black ground. What makes us perceive it as the one or the other? A gardener would perhaps be more likely to see it as the flower, and a military man as the cross. Perception depends upon this pre-existent element of choice, which determines the form in which we perceive not only all the varieties of geometrical figures but every phenomenon of which we become aware. What is perceived is not the reflection of something objective which the mind duplicates within itself; it is the result of that something and of the mind's percipient activity; and this again is a function of some tension or tendency towards a certain goal. (It is easy to see the relation of this to psychoanalysis, the Adlerian much more than the Freudian.) There is, therefore, no objectivity. Or if there is, it can only reside in the knowledge of the possible forms of perception, of all their relations and interdependencies, which may be reducible to certain basic formulae and might represent, in sum, the knowledge of the perceiving subject as a whole, of a transcendental knower, in and by which (or whom) all our perceiving takes place. This is, one gathers, the aim of the pure phenomenologists. Their work, although it starts from descriptive data, often provided by experiments, is clearly in the straight Kantian tradition. But the perceptual element being set in motion, as it were, by a dynamic or vitalistic notion of it, and balanced eternally on this edge of "choice," this very abstract tradition of speculative thought is now carried on by Heidegger into the study of passionate humanity in our turbulent world — rather to the displeasure of his master Husserl.

Heidegger knows, as did Kierkegaard, the intensity of man's anxiety to feel and know that he exists, and that this is the root of all his anxieties. If — as phenomenology demonstrates — we do not know objects, nor do we know ourselves the subjects, if we know only phenomena which are the transitory and contingent products of the interaction of these two "unknowns" — then, to be born into this life is to find oneself pitched into the drift of phenomena, "abandoned," — "responsible" for our

Introduction

existence and yet ever more clearly realising to our "anguish" that the whole is meaningless.¹ In the remedy proposed by Heidegger, there is a somewhat Nietzschean flavour. The only hope for man lies in his full realisation and acceptance of the truth "that these things are not otherwise but thus." And although his personal fate is simply to perish, he can triumph over it by inventing "purposes," "projects," which will themselves confer meaning both upon himself and upon the world of objects —all meaningless otherwise and in themselves. There is indeed no reason why a man should do this, and he gets nothing by it except the authentic knowledge that he exists; but that precisely is his great, his transcendent need and desire. Not many are capable thus of authenticating their existence: the great majority reassure themselves by thinking as little as possible of their approaching deaths and by worshipping idols such as humanity, science, or some objective divinity.

This pitiless atheism, relieved by a tenuous thread of heroism, is canonical doctrine to the French existentialists of the school of Sartre. But there are other protagonists

---

1 All these words, with these or closely related meanings, recur in the present lecture of M. Sartre.

of existentialism in that country, among them the philosopher and dramatist Gabriel Marcel, whose arrival at the existential position was completed by his conversion to the Roman Catholic communion. Marcel owes more to Nietzsche than to Heidegger, much of course directly to Kierkegaard and most of all to his own French philosophic tradition. And the stream of existentialism in France has been swollen from a number of tributaries arising from more distant sources; such names as Chestov, Berdiaieff and even Kafka, to name no more, often recur in existentialist literature, as those of writers who have had the same or similar insights into the present crisis and the menace it presents to subjective existence. This variety of testimonies, whilst it confirms existentialism as a spontaneous movement in contemporary European thought, does less than nothing to clarify its political and religious ambiguities. But its very indeterminism in this respect is what has enabled existentialism to provide a forum and a language in which various religious, secular idealist and anti-religious advocates can and do meet to discuss human problems of primary importance and common concern.

The performance of this function, which is made possible by the intense personalism of the existential

Introduction

method, justifies M. Sartre in defending this philosophy as humanist. Actually, it is as much a reform as a form of humanism. To the originators of that tradition man was born "good" or at least was ethically neutral until corrupt philosophy and inequitable institutions perverted his will—a conception that is untenable since the epoch of psychoanalysis and unthinkable in terms derived through Kierkegaard, Nietzsche and Heidegger. The humanism of the contemporary existentialists is decidedly disillusioned and of a profound ethical tension not least in the case of M. Sartre whose ethic of action is the Kantian one of universal validity insofar as the agent can estimate it. But M. Sartre's working criterion of the unethical is very near to the religious description of sin. Unethical action, he says, is always characterised by that contradiction of the self by itself which he calls *mauvaise foi*.[2] At this point secular idealism and religious tradition

---

[2] *Mauvaise foi* is one of the cardinal concepts in Sartrean existentialism, very precisely illustrated elsewhere in M. Sartre's works by concrete instances. I have nearly always translated it as "self-deception," which seems preferable to the literal rendering of the words and slightly closer to their meaning.

Another important Sartrean concept—*engagement*—is here translated as "commitment" for the similar reason that the French word used by the author conveys a shade of meaning different from that of our word "engagement"; the existentialism *engagement* is essentially unilateral.

have been, at least for the moment, brought into close accord by the analytic psychologists also—in their perception that nothing in man is so individual (in the sense of isolation) as his feeling of guilt.

But if what is most subjective is thus what is in general, also most secret, how does existential philosophy obtain its essential material? It is by the provision of this material for its studies that existentialism has become a practical philosophy for the first time in France; not so much in the sense that groups of individuals in France try to live by its light, though that is said to be the case, but because the French are an artistic people able to provide material in fictional form. A doctrine resting upon individual subjectivity whose existence is prior to its essence, needs descriptions of such subjectivities to substantiate its theme; and except so far as the existential subject himself supplies these—as Kierkegaard does, and Marcel and others to some degree—they can only be competently substituted by the intuition of artists. Art is, indeed, a fundamental concern of Kierkegaard, who thought that any man who was not either religious or an artist must be a fool: though how far Kierkegaard would have been willing to trust artists to supply reliable accounts of human subjective happenings is another matter. But

Introduction

such intuitive and imaginative accounts, whatever their reliability, are being abundantly provided in France, and have made possible the sudden and wide diffusion of existential knowledge—at the least of its terms and categories—in otherwise unlikely quarters. French existentialism is substantially due to the work of literary artists and M. Sartre's own exposition of it is inseparable from his eminent contribution to letters as a novelist.

No one can yet prophesy the outcome or ultimate value of such a movement. The vigorous opposition it has provoked, some of which is of philosophical and critical value, is one of the signs of its vitality: and one has only to begin to trace its origins and observe reactions to it, to realise how deeply it is rooted in the recent cultural history of Europe, not to mention its conscious affinities with movements much further back which were highly creative in effect. In the discussion that follows the present lecture, the discerning reader will notice that several recent disturbances in Western thinking—the impacts of indeterminism upon science, of the analytic method upon psychology, of scepticism upon historicity, phenomenology upon philosophy—are all brought to focus in this most radical and realistic way of thinking. Neither its complete modernity nor its representative character can be doubted, and its future is viewed with concern, hopeful or otherwise, by some at least who have discerning eyes for the movements that matter.

Much of it, though not all, could easily peter out in *vulgarisation*—not only in the French, but the less respectable English sense of the word. And there is an inherent reason why decision on this point can hardly be long delayed. A philosophy in which "choice," in the sense of a crisis of the subjectivity, plays a dominant role, is a philosophy of conversion. Essentially considered its subjectivity may be pure and unalloyed, but viewed externally the protagonists are evangelists *for* something, and conversions happening under their influence must have an objective side or they are not even existential. This could, indeed, be a cause of spurious adherents whose existentialism might be instrumental to designs of more concretely proselytising character. But that would be only a complication of the problem which is a very real one, and even genuine existentialism seems unlikely to solve it. Indeed, it is probably insoluble.

The "conversional" tendency in M. Sartre's lecture is towards a political activity which in the eyes of most others—such as his interlocutor, M. Naville, for instance —would be incompatible with the essential value in the

Introduction

doctrine he holds. To him freedom is the value of all values. It is as a philosopher of freedom that M. Sartre's contribution to existentialism is most brilliant and does most honour to the enlightened traditions of his country: but he has not yet worked out for himself the political implications of a philosophy of absolute freedom. Nor does he seem yet to have developed their subjective consequences either as deeply or as far as Kierkegaard, still less beyond him. If he did this it may be, as Professor Saurat observed, that the philosophic necessities inherent in his fundamental premise would carry him towards a theistic position. It is at least evident that he is raising precisely the questions which so many of this age are anxious, in the name of dogmatic scientism, to suppress.

PHILIP MAIRET

Existentialism
and Humanism

My purpose here is to offer a defence of existentialism against several reproaches that have been laid against it.

First, it has been reproached as an invitation to people to dwell in quietism of despair. For if every way to a solution is barred, one would have to regard any action in this world as entirely ineffective, and one would arrive finally at a contemplative philosophy. Moreover, since contemplation is a luxury, this would be only another bourgeois philosophy. This is, especially, the reproach made by the Communists.

From another quarter we are reproached for having underlined all that is ignominious in the human situation, for depicting what is mean, sordid or base to the neglect of certain things that possess charm and beauty and belong to the brighter side of human nature: for example, according to the Catholic critic, Mlle. Mercier, we forget how an infant smiles. Both from this side and from the other we are also reproached for leaving out of account the solidarity of mankind and considering man in isolation. And this, say the Communists, is because we base our doctrine upon pure subjectivity—upon the Cartesian "I think": which is the moment in which solitary man attains to himself; a position from which it is impossible to regain solidarity with other men who exist outside of the self. The *ego* cannot reach them through the *cogito*.

From the Christian side, we are reproached as people who deny the reality and seriousness of human affairs. For since we ignore the commandments of God and all values prescribed as eternal, nothing remains but what is strictly voluntary. Everyone can do what he likes, and will be incapable, from such a point of view, of condemning either the point of view or the action of anyone else.

It is to these various reproaches that I shall endeavour to reply today; that is why I have entitled this brief exposition "Existentialism and Humanism." Many may be surprised at the mention of humanism in this connection, but we shall try to see in what sense we understand it. In any case, we can begin by saying that existentialism, in our sense of the word, is a doctrine that does render human life possible; a doctrine, also, which affirms that every truth and every action imply both an environment and a human subjectivity. The essential charge laid against us is, of course, that of over-emphasis upon the evil side of human life. I have lately been told of a lady who, whenever she lets slip a vulgar expression in a moment of nervousness, excuses herself by exclaiming, "I believe I am becoming an existentialist." So it appears that ugliness is being identified with existentialism. That is why some people say we are "naturalistic," and if we are, it is strange to see how much we scandalise and horrify them, for no one seems to be much frightened or humiliated nowadays by what is properly called naturalism. Those who can quite well keep down a novel by Zola such as *La Terre* are sickened as soon as they read an existentialist novel. Those who appeal to the wisdom of the people—which is a sad wisdom—find ours sadder still. And yet, what could be more disillusioned than such sayings as "Charity begins at home" or "Promote a rogue and he'll sue you for damage, knock him down and he'll do you homage"?[3] We all know how many common sayings can be quoted to this effect, and they all mean much the same—that you must not oppose the powers-that-be; that you must not fight against superior force; must

---

3 *Oignez vilain il vous plaindra, poignez vilain il vous oindra.*

not meddle in matters that are above your station. Or that any action not in accordance with some tradition is mere romanticism; or that any undertaking which has not the support of proven experience is foredoomed to frustration; and that since experience has shown men to be invariably inclined to evil, there must be firm rules to restrain them, otherwise we shall have anarchy. It is, however, the people who are forever mouthing these dismal proverbs and, whenever they are told of some more or less repulsive action, say "How like human nature!"—it is these very people, always harping upon realism, who complain that existentialism is too gloomy a view of things. Indeed their excessive protests make me suspect that what is annoying them is not so much our pessimism, but, much more likely, our optimism. For at bottom, what is alarming in the doctrine that I am about to try to explain to you is—is it not?—that it confronts man with a possibility of choice. To verify this, let us review the whole question upon the strictly philosophic level. What, then, is this that we call existentialism?

Most of those who are making use of this word would be highly confused if required to explain its meaning. For since it has become fashionable, people cheerfully declare that this musician or that painter is "existentialist." A

Existentialism and Humanism

columnist in *Clartés* signs himself "The Existentialist," and, indeed, the word is now so loosely applied to so many things that it no longer means anything at all. It would appear that, for the lack of any novel doctrine such as that of surrealism, all those who are eager to join in the latest scandal or movement now seize upon this philosophy in which, however, they can find nothing to their purpose. For in truth this is of all teachings the least scandalous and the most austere: it is intended strictly for technicians and philosophers. All the same, it can easily be defined.

The question is only complicated because there are two kinds of existentialists. There are, on the one hand, the Christians, amongst whom I shall name Jaspers and Gabriel Marcel, both professed Catholics; and on the other the existential atheists, amongst whom we must place Heidegger as well as the French existentialists and myself. What they have in common is simply the fact that they believe that *existence* comes before *essence*—or, if you will, that we must begin from the subjective. What exactly do we mean by that?

If one considers an article of manufacture—as, for example, a book or a paper-knife—one sees that it has been made by an artisan who had a conception of it; and

Jean-Paul Sartre

he has paid attention, equally, to the conception of a paper-knife and to the pre-existent technique of production which is a part of that conception and is, at bottom, a formula. Thus the paper-knife is at the same time an article producible in a certain manner and one which, on the other hand, serves a definite purpose, for one cannot suppose that a man would produce a paperknife without knowing what it was for. Let us say, then, of the paper-knife that its essence—that is to say the sum of the formulae and the qualities which made its production and its definition possible—precedes its existence. The presence of such-and-such a paper-knife or book is thus determined before my eyes. Here, then, we are viewing the world from a technical standpoint, and we can say that production precedes existence.

When we think of God as the creator, we are thinking of him, most of the time, as a supernal artisan. Whatever doctrine we may be considering, whether it be a doctrine like that of Descartes, or of Leibnitz himself, we always imply that the will follows, more or less, from the understanding or at least accompanies it, so that when God creates he knows precisely what he is creating. Thus, the conception of man in the mind of God is comparable to that of the paper-knife in the mind of the artisan: God makes man according to a procedure and a conception, exactly as the artisan manufactures a paper-knife, following a definition and a formula. Thus each individual man is the realisation of a certain conception which dwells in the divine understanding. In the philosophic atheism of the eighteenth century, the notion of God is suppressed, but not, for all that, the idea that essence is prior to existence; something of that idea we still find everywhere, in Diderot, in Voltaire and even in Kant. Man possesses a human nature; that "human nature," which is the conception of human being, is found in every man; which means that each man is a particular example of an universal conception, the conception of Man. In Kant, this universality goes so far that the wild man of the woods, man in the state of nature and the bourgeois are all contained in the same definition and have the same fundamental qualities. Here again, the essence of man precedes that historic existence which we confront in experience.

Atheistic existentialism, of which I am a representative, declares with greater consistency that if God does not exist there is at least one being whose existence comes before its essence, a being which exists before it can be defined by any conception of it. That being is man or, as Heidegger has it, the human reality. What do we mean by

Jean-Paul Sartre

saying that existence precedes essence? We mean that man first of all exists, encounters himself, surges up in the world—and defines himself afterwards. If man as the existentialist sees him is not definable, it is because to begin with he is nothing. He will not be anything until later, and then he will be what he makes of himself. Thus, there is no human nature, because there is no God to have a conception of it. Man simply is. Not that he is simply what he conceives himself to be but he is what he wills, and as he conceives himself after already existing—as he wills to be after that leap towards existence. Man is nothing else but that which he makes of himself. That is the first principle of existentialism. And this is what people call its "subjectivity," using the word as a reproach against us. But what do we mean to say by this, but that man is of a greater dignity than a stone or a table? For we mean to say that man primarily exists—that man is, before all else, something which propels itself towards a future and is aware that it is doing so. Man is, indeed, a project which possesses a subjective life, instead of being a kind of moss, or a fungus or a cauliflower. Before that projection of the self nothing exists; not even in the heaven of intelligence: man will only attain existence when he is what he purposes to be. Not, however, what he may wish to be. For what we usually understand by wishing or willing is a conscious decision taken—much more often than not—after we have made ourselves what we are. I may wish to join a party, to write a book or to marry—but in such a case what is usually called my will is probably a manifestation of a prior and more spontaneous decision. If, however, it is true that existence is prior to essence, man is responsible for what he is. Thus, the first effect of existentialism is that it puts every man in possession of himself as he is, and places the entire responsibility for his existence squarely upon his own shoulders. And, when we say that man is responsible for himself, we do not mean that he is responsible only for his own individuality, but that he is responsible for all men. The word "subjectivism" is to be understood in two senses, and our adversaries play upon only one of them. Subjectivism means, on the one hand, the freedom of the individual subject and, on the other, that man cannot pass beyond human subjectivity. It is the latter which is the deeper meaning of existentialism. When we say that man chooses himself, we do mean that every one of us must choose himself; but by that we also mean that in choosing for himself he chooses for all men. For in effect, of all the actions a man may take in order to create himself as he wills to be, there is not one which is not creative, at the same time, of an image of man such as he believes he ought to be. To choose between this or that is at the same time to affirm the value of that which is chosen; for we are unable ever to choose the worse. What we choose is always the better; and nothing can be better for us unless it is better for all. If, moreover, existence precedes essence and we will to exist at the same time as we fashion our image, that image is valid for all and for the entire epoch in which we find ourselves. Our responsibility is thus much greater than we had supposed, for it concerns mankind as a whole. If I am a worker, for instance, I may choose to join a Christian rather than a Communist trade union. And if, by that membership, I choose to signify that resignation is, after all, the attitude that best becomes a man, that man's kingdom is not upon this earth, I do not commit myself alone to that view. Resignation is my will for everyone, and my action is, in consequence, a commitment on behalf of all mankind. Or if, to take a more personal case, I decide to marry and to have children, even though this decision proceeds simply from my situation, from my passion or my desire, I am thereby committing not only myself, but humanity as a whole, to the practice of monogamy. I am thus

Existentialism and Humanism

responsible for myself and for all men, and I am creating a certain image of man as I would have him to be. In fashioning myself I fashion man.

This may enable us to understand what is meant by such terms—perhaps a little grandiloquent—as anguish, abandonment and despair. As you will soon see, it is very simple. First, what do we mean by anguish? The existentialist frankly states that man is in anguish. His meaning is as follows—When a man commits himself to anything, fully realising that he is not only choosing what he will be, but is thereby at the same time a legislator deciding for the whole of mankind—in such a moment a man cannot escape from the sense of complete and profound responsibility. There are many, indeed, who show no such anxiety. But we affirm that they are merely disguising their anguish or are in flight from it. Certainly, many people think that in what they are doing they commit no one but themselves to anything: and if you ask them, "What would happen if everyone did so?" they shrug their shoulders and reply, "Everyone does not do so." But in truth, one ought always to ask oneself what would happen if everyone did as one is doing; nor can one escape from that disturbing thought except by a kind of self-deception. The man who lies in self-excuse, by saying "Everyone will not do it" must be ill at ease in his conscience, for the act of lying implies the universal value which it denies. By its very disguise his anguish reveals itself. This is the anguish that Kierkegaard called "the anguish of Abraham." You know the story: An angel commanded Abraham to sacrifice his son: and obedience was obligatory, if it really was an angel who had appeared and said, "Thou, Abraham, shalt sacrifice thy son." But anyone in such a case would wonder, first, whether it was indeed an angel and secondly, whether I am really Abraham. Where are the proofs? A certain mad woman who suffered from hallucinations said that people were telephoning to her, and giving her orders. The doctor asked, "But who is it that speaks to you?" She replied: "He says it is God." And what, indeed, could prove to her that it was God? If an angel appears to me, what is the proof that it is an angel; or, if I hear voices, who can prove that they proceed from heaven and not from hell, or from my own subconsciousness or some pathological condition? Who can prove that they are really addressed to me?

Who, then, can prove that I am the proper person to impose, by my own choice, my conception of man upon mankind? I shall never find any proof whatever; there will be no sign to convince me of it. If a voice speaks to me, it is still I myself who must decide whether the voice is or is not that of an angel. If I regard a certain course of action as good, it is only I who choose to say that it is good and not bad. There is nothing to show that I am Abraham: nevertheless I also am obliged at every instant to perform actions which are examples. Everything happens to every man as though the whole human race had its eyes fixed upon what he is doing and regulated its conduct accordingly. So every man ought to say, "Am I really a man who has the right to act in such a manner that humanity regulates itself by what I do." If a man does not say that, he is dissembling his anguish. Clearly, the anguish with which we are concerned here is not one that could lead to quietism or inaction. It is anguish pure and simple, of the kind well known to all those who have borne responsibilities. When, for instance, a military leader takes upon himself the responsibility for an attack and sends a number of men to their death, he chooses to do it and at bottom he alone chooses. No doubt he acts under a higher command, but its orders, which are more general, require interpretation by him and upon that interpretation depends the life of ten, fourteen or twenty men. In making the decision, he cannot but feel a certain anguish. All leaders know that anguish. It does not prevent their acting, on the contrary it is the very condition of their action, for the action presupposes that there is a plurality of possibilities, and in choosing one of these, they realise that it has value only because it is chosen. Now it is anguish of that kind which existentialism describes, and moreover, as we shall see, makes explicit through direct responsibility towards other men who are concerned. Far from being a screen which could separate us from action, it is a condition of action itself.

And when we speak of "abandonment"—a favourite word of Heidegger—we only mean to say that God does not exist, and that it is necessary to draw the consequences of his absence right to the end. The existentialist is strongly opposed to a certain type of secular moralism which seeks to suppress God at the least possible expense. Towards 1880, when the French professors endeavoured to formulate a secular morality, they said something like this:—God is a useless and costly hypothesis, so we will do without it. However, if we are to have morality, a society and a law-abiding world, it is essential that certain values should be taken seriously; they must have *à priori* existence ascribed to them. It must be considered obligatory *à priori* to be honest, not to lie, not to beat one's wife, to bring up children and so forth; so we are going to do a little work on this subject, which will enable us to show that these values exist all the same, inscribed in an intelligible heaven although, of course, there is no God. In other words—and this is, I believe, the purport of all that we in France call radicalism—nothing will be changed if God does not exist; we shall rediscover the same norms of honesty, progress and humanity, and we shall have disposed of God as an out-of-date hypothesis which will die away quietly of itself. The existentialist, on the contrary, finds it extremely embarrassing that God does not exist, for there disappears with Him all possibility of finding values in an intelligible heaven. There can no longer be any good *à priori*, since there is no infinite and perfect consciousness to think it. It is nowhere written that "the good" exists, that one must be honest or must not lie, since we are now upon the plane where there are only men. Dostoievsky once wrote "If God did not exist, everything would be permitted"; and that, for existentialism, is the starting point. Everything is indeed permitted if God does not exist, and man is in consequence forlorn, for he cannot find anything to depend upon either within or outside himself. He discovers forthwith, that he is without excuse. For if indeed existence precedes essence, one will never be able to explain one's action by reference to a given and specific human nature; in other words, there is no determinism—man is free, man is freedom. Nor, on the other hand, if God does not exist, are we provided with any values or commands that could legitimise our behaviour. Thus we have neither behind us, nor before us in a luminous realm of values, any means of justification or excuse. We are left alone, without excuse. That is what I mean when I say that man is condemned to be free. Condemned, because he did not create himself, yet is nevertheless at liberty, and from the moment that he is thrown into this world he is responsible for everything he does. The existentialist does not believe in the power of passion. He will never regard a grand passion as a destructive torrent upon which a man is swept into certain actions as by fate, and which, therefore, is an excuse for them. He thinks that man is responsible for his passion. Neither will an existentialist think that a man can find help through some sign being vouchsafed upon earth for his orientation: for he thinks that the man himself interprets the sign as he chooses. He thinks that every man, without any support or help whatever, is condemned at every instant to invent man. As Ponge has written in a very fine article, "Man is the future of man." That is exactly true. Only, if one took this to mean that the future is laid up in Heaven, that God knows what it is, it would be false, for then it would no longer even be a future. If, however, it means that, whatever man may now appear to be, there is a future to be fashioned, a virgin future that awaits him — then it is a true saying. But in the present one is forsaken.

As an example by which you may the better understand this state of abandonment, I will refer to the case of a pupil of mine, who sought me out in the following circumstances. His father was quarrelling with his mother and was also inclined to be a "collaborator"; his elder brother had been killed in the German offensive of 1940 and this young man, with a sentiment somewhat primitive but generous, burned to avenge him. His mother was living alone with him, deeply afflicted by the semi-treason of his father and by the death of her eldest son, and her one consolation was in this young man. But he, at this moment, had the choice between going to England to join the Free French Forces or of staying near his mother and helping her to live. He fully realised that this woman lived only for him and that his disappearance — or perhaps his death — would plunge her into despair. He also realised that, concretely and in fact, every action he performed on his mother's behalf would be sure of effect in the sense of aiding her to live, whereas anything he did in order to go and fight would be an ambiguous action which might vanish like water into sand and serve no purpose. For instance, to set out for England he would have to wait indefinitely in a Spanish camp on the way through Spain; or, on arriving in England or in Algiers he might be put into an office to fill up forms. Consequently, he found himself confronted by two very different modes of action; the one concrete, immediate, but directed towards only one individual; and the other an action addressed to an end infinitely greater, a national collectivity, but for that very reason ambiguous—and it might be frustrated on the way. At the same time, he was hesitating between two kinds of morality; on the one side the morality of sympathy, of personal devotion and, on the other side, a morality of wider scope but of more debatable validity. He had to choose between those two. What could help him to choose? Could the Christian doctrine? No. Christian doctrine says: Act with charity, love your neighbour, deny yourself for others, choose the way which is hardest, and so forth. But which is the harder road? To whom does one owe the more brotherly love, the patriot or the mother? Which is the more useful aim, the general one of fighting in and for the whole community, or the precise aim of helping one particular person to live? Who can give an answer to that *à priori*? No one. Nor is it given in any ethical scripture. The Kantian ethic says, Never regard another as a means, but always as an end. Very well; if I remain with my mother, I shall be regarding her as the end and not as a means: but by the same token I am in danger of treating as means those who are fighting on my behalf; and the converse is also true, that if I go to the aid of the combatants I shall be treating them as the end at the risk of treating my mother as a means.

If values are uncertain, if they are still too abstract to determine the particular, concrete case under consideration, nothing remains but to trust in our instincts. That is what this young man tried to do; and when I saw him he said, "In the end, it is feeling that counts; the direction in which it is really pushing me is the one I ought to choose. If I feel that I love my mother enough to sacrifice everything else for her—my will to be avenged, all my longings for action and adventure—then I stay with her. If, on the contrary, I feel that my love for her is not enough, I go." But how does one estimate the strength of a feeling? The value of his feeling for his mother was determined precisely by the fact that he was standing by her. I may say that I love a certain friend enough to sacrifice such or such a sum of money for him, but I cannot prove that unless I have done it. I may say, "I love my mother enough to remain with her," if actually I have remained with her. I can only estimate the strength of this affection if I have performed an action by which it is defined and ratified. But if I then appeal to this affection to justify my action, I find myself drawn into a vicious circle.

Moreover, as Gide has very well said, a sentiment which is play-acting and one which is vital are two things that are hardly distinguishable one from another. To decide that I love my mother by staying beside her, and to play a comedy the upshot of which is that I do so—these are nearly the same thing. In other words, feeling is formed by the deeds that one does; therefore I cannot consult it as a guide to action. And that is to say that I can neither seek within myself for an authentic impulse to action, nor can I expect, from some ethic, formulae that will enable me to act. You may say that the youth did, at least, go to a professor to ask for advice. But if you seek counsel—from a priest, for example—you have selected that priest; and at bottom you already knew, more or less, what he would advise. In other words, to choose an adviser is nevertheless to commit oneself by that choice. If you are a Christian, you will say, "Consult a priest"; but there are collaborationists, priests who are resisters and priests who wait for the tide to turn: which will you choose? Had this young man chosen a priest of the resistance, or one of the collaboration, he would have decided beforehand the kind of advice he was to receive. Similarly, in coming to me, he knew what advice I should give him, and I had but one reply to make. You are free, therefore choose — that is to say, invent. No rule of general morality can show you what you ought to do: no signs are vouchsafed in this world. The Catholics will reply, "Oh, but they are!" Very well; still, it is I myself, in every case, who have to interpret the signs. Whilst I was imprisoned, I made the acquaintance of a somewhat remarkable man, a Jesuit, who had become a member of that order in the following manner. In his life he had suffered a succession of rather severe setbacks. His father had died when he was a child, leaving him in poverty, and he had been awarded a free scholarship in a religious institution, where he had been made continually to feel that he was accepted for charity's sake, and, in consequence, he had been denied several of those distinctions and honours which gratify children. Later, about the age of eighteen, he came to grief in a sentimental affair; and finally, at twenty-two—this was a trifle in itself, but it was the last drop that overflowed his cup—he failed in his military examination. This young man, then, could regard himself as a total failure: it was a sign—but a sign of what? He might have taken refuge in bitterness or despair. But he took it—very cleverly for him—as a sign that he was not intended for secular successes, and that only the attainments of religion, those of sanctity and of faith, were accessible to him. He interpreted his record as a message from God, and became a member of the Order. Who can doubt but that this decision as to the meaning of the sign was his, and his alone? One could have drawn quite different conclusions from such a series of reverses—as, for example, that he had better become a carpenter or a revolutionary. For the decipherment of the sign, however, he bears the entire responsibility. That is what "abandonment" implies, that we ourselves decide our being. And with this abandonment goes anguish.

As for "despair," the meaning of this expression is extremely simple. It merely means that we limit ourselves to a reliance upon that which is within our wills, or within the sum of the probabilities which render our action feasible. Whenever one wills anything, there are always these elements of probability. If I am counting upon a visit from a friend, who may be coming by train or by tram, I presuppose that the train will arrive at the appointed time, or that the tram will not be derailed. I remain in the realm of possibilities; but one does not rely upon any possibilities beyond those that are strictly concerned in one's action. Beyond the point at which the possibilities under consideration cease to affect my action, I ought to disinterest myself. For there is no God and no prevenient design, which can adapt the world and all its possibilities to my will. When Descartes said, "Conquer yourself rather than the world," what he meant was, at bottom, the same—that we should act without hope.

Marxists, to whom I have said this, have answered: "Your action is limited, obviously, by your death; but you can rely upon the help of others. That is, you can count both upon what the others are doing to help you elsewhere, as in China and in Russia, and upon what they will do later, after your death, to take up your action and carry it forward to its final accomplishment which will be the revolution. Moreover you must rely upon this; not to do so is immoral." To this I rejoin, first, that I shall always count upon my comrades-in-arms in the struggle, in so far as they are committed, as I am, to a definite, common cause; and in the unity of a party or a group which I can more or less control—that is, in which I am enrolled as a militant and whose movements at every moment are known to me. In that respect, to rely upon the unity and the will of the party is exactly like my reckoning that the train will run to time or that the tram will not be derailed. But I cannot count upon men whom I do not know, I cannot base my confidence upon human goodness or upon man's interest in the good of society, seeing that man is free and that there is no human nature which I can take as foundational. I do not know whither the Russian revolution will lead. I can admire it and take it as an example in so far as it is evident, today, that the proletariat plays a part in Russia which it has attained in no other nation. But I cannot affirm that this will necessarily lead to the triumph of the proletariat: I must confine myself to what I can see. Nor can I be sure that comrades-in-arms will take up my work after my death and carry it to the maximum perfection, seeing that those men are free agents and will freely decide, tomorrow, what man is then to be. Tomorrow, after my death, some men may decide to establish Fascism, and the others may be so cowardly or so slack as to let them do so. If so, Fascism will then be the truth of man, and so much the worse for us. In reality, things will be such as men have decided they shall be. Does that mean that I should abandon myself to quietism? No. First I ought to commit myself and then act my commitment, according to the time-honoured formula that "one need not hope in order to undertake one's work." Nor does this mean that I should not belong to a party, but only that I should be without illusion and that I should do what I can. For instance, if I ask myself "Will the social ideal as such, ever become a reality?" I cannot tell, I only know that whatever may be in my power to make it so, I shall do; beyond that, I can count upon nothing.

Quietism is the attitude of people who say, "let others do what I cannot do." The doctrine I am presenting before you is precisely the opposite of this, since it declares that there is no reality except in action. It goes further, indeed, and adds, "Man is nothing else but what he purposes, he exists only in so far as he realises himself, he is therefore nothing else but the sum of his actions, nothing else but what his life is." Hence we can well understand why some people are horrified by our teaching. For many have but one resource to sustain them in their misery, and that is to think, "Circumstances have been against me, I was worthy to be something much better than I have been. I admit I have never had a great love or a great friendship; but that is because I never met a man or a woman who were worthy of it; if I have not written any very good books, it is because I had not the leisure to do so; or, if I have had no children to whom I could devote myself it is because I did not find the man I could have lived with. So there remains within me a wide range of abilities, inclinations and potentialities, unused but perfectly viable, which endow me with a worthiness that could never be inferred from the mere history of my actions." But in reality and for the existentialist, there is no love apart from the deeds of love; no potentiality of love other than that which is manifested in loving; there is no genius other than that which is expressed in works of art. The genius of Proust is the totality of the works of Proust; the genius of Racine is the series of his tragedies, outside of which there is nothing. Why should we attribute to Racine the capacity to write yet another tragedy when that is precisely what he did not write? In life, a man commits himself, draws his own portrait and there is nothing but that portrait. No doubt this thought may seem comfortless to one who has not made a success of his life. On the other hand, it puts everyone in a position to understand that reality alone is reliable; that dreams, expectations and hopes serve to define a man only as deceptive dreams, abortive hopes, expectations unfulfilled; that is to say, they define him negatively, not positively. Nevertheless, when one says, "You are nothing else but what you live," it does not imply that an artist is to be judged solely by his works of art, for a thousand other things contribute no less to his definition as a man. What we mean to say is that a man is no other than a series of undertakings, that he is the sum, the organisation, the set of relations that constitute these undertakings.

In the light of all this, what people reproach us with is not, after all, our pessimism, but the sternness of our optimism. If people condemn our works of fiction in which we describe characters that are base, weak, cowardly and sometimes even frankly evil, it is not only because those characters are base, weak, cowardly or evil. For suppose that, like Zola, we showed that the behaviour of these characters was caused by their heredity, or by the action of their environment upon them, or by determining factors, psychic or organic. People would be reassured, they would say, "You see, that is what we are like, no one can do anything about it." But the existentialist, when he portrays a coward, shows him as responsible for his

Jean-Paul Sartre

cowardice. He is not like that on account of a cowardly heart or lungs or cerebrum, he has not become like that through his physiological organism; he is like that because he has made himself into a coward by his actions. There is no such thing as a cowardly temperament. There are nervous temperaments; there is what is called impoverished blood, and there are also rich temperaments. But the man whose blood is poor is not a coward for all that, for what produces cowardice is the act of giving up or giving way; and a temperament is not an action. A coward is defined by the deed that he has done. What people feel obscurely, and with horror, is that the coward as we present him is guilty of being a coward. What people would prefer would be to be born either a coward or a hero. One of the charges most often laid against the *Chemins de la Liberté* is something like this — "But, after all, these people being so base, how can you make them into heroes?" That objection is really rather comic, for it implies that people are born heroes: and that is, at bottom, what such people would like to think. If you are born cowards, you can be quite content, you can do nothing about it and you will be cowards all your lives whatever you do; and if you are born heroes you can again be quite content; you will be heroes all your lives, eating and drinking heroically. Whereas the existentialist says that the coward makes himself cowardly, the hero makes himself heroic; and that there is always a possibility for the coward to give up cowardice and for the hero to stop being a hero. What counts is the total commitment, and it is not by a particular case or particular action that you are committed altogether.

We have now, I think, dealt with a certain number of the reproaches against existentialism. You have seen that it cannot be regarded as a philosophy of quietism since it defines man by his action; nor as a pessimistic description of man, for no doctrine is more optimistic, the destiny of man is placed within himself. Nor is it an attempt to discourage man from action since it tells him that there is no hope except in his action, and that the one thing which permits him to have life is the deed. Upon this level therefore, what we are considering is an ethic of action and self-commitment. However, we are still reproached, upon these few data, for confining man within his individual subjectivity. There again people badly misunderstand us.

Our point of departure is, indeed, the subjectivity of the individual, and that for strictly philosophic reasons. It is not because we are bourgeois, but because we seek to base our teaching upon the truth, and not upon a collection of fine theories, full of hope but lacking real foundations. And at the point of departure there cannot be any other truth than this, *I think, therefore I am*, which is the absolute truth of consciousness as it attains to itself. Every theory which begins with man, outside of this moment of self-attainment, is a theory which thereby suppresses the truth, for outside of the Cartesian *cogito*, all objects are no more than probable, and any doctrine of probabilities which is not attached to a truth will crumble into nothing. In order to define the probable one must possess the true. Before there can be any truth whatever, then, there must be an absolute truth, and there is such a truth which is simple, easily attained and within the reach of everybody; it consists in one's immediate sense of one's self.

In the second place, this theory alone is compatible with the dignity of man, it is the only one which does not make man into an object. All kinds of materialism lead one to treat every man including oneself as an object—that is, as a set of pre-determined reactions, in no way different from the patterns of qualities and phenomena which constitute a table, or a chair or a stone. Our aim is precisely to establish the human kingdom as a pattern of values in distinction from the material world. But the subjectivity which we thus postulate as the standard of truth is no narrowly individual subjectivism, for as we have demonstrated, it is not only one's own self that one discovers in the *cogito*, but those of others too. Contrary to the philosophy of Descartes, contrary to that of Kant, when we say "I think" we are attaining to ourselves in the presence of the other, and we are just as certain of the other as we are of ourselves. Thus the man who discovers himself directly in the *cogito* also discovers all the others, and discovers them as the condition of his own existence. He recognises that he cannot be anything (in the sense in which one says one is spiritual, or that one is wicked or jealous) unless others recognise him as such. I cannot obtain any truth whatsoever about myself, except through the mediation of another. The other is indispensable to my existence, and equally so to any knowledge I can have of myself. Under these conditions, the intimate discovery of myself is at the same time the revelation of the other as a freedom which confronts mine, and which cannot think or will without doing so either for or against me. Thus, at once, we find ourselves in a world which is, let us say, that of "inter-subjectivity." It is in this world that man has to decide what he is and what others are.

Furthermore, although it is impossible to find in each and every man a universal essence that can be called human nature, there is nevertheless a human universality of *condition*. It is not by chance that the thinkers of today are so much more ready to speak of the condition than of the nature of man. By his condition they understand, with more or less clarity, all the *limitations* which *à priori* define man's fundamental situation in the universe. His historical situations are variable: man may be born a slave in a pagan society, or may be a feudal baron, or a proletarian. But what never vary are the necessities of being in the world, of having to labour and to die there. These limitations are neither subjective nor objective, or rather there is both a subjective and an objective aspect of them. Objective, because we meet with them everywhere and they are everywhere recognisable: and subjective because they are *lived* and are nothing if man does not live them — if, that is to say, he does not freely determine himself and his existence in relation to them. And, diverse though man's purposes may be, at least none of them is wholly foreign to me, since every human purpose presents itself as an attempt either to surpass these limitations, or to widen them, or else to deny or to accommodate oneself to them. Consequently every purpose, however individual it may be, is of universal value. Every purpose, even that of a Chinese, an Indian or a Negro, can be understood by a European. To say it can be understood, means that the European of 1945 may be striving out of a certain situation towards the same limitations in the same way, and that he may reconceive in himself the purpose of the Chinese of the Indian or the African. In every purpose there is universality, in this sense that every purpose is comprehensible to every man. Not that this or that purpose defines man for ever, but that it may be entertained again and again. There is always some way of understanding an idiot, a child, a primitive man or a foreigner if one has sufficient information. In this sense we may say that there is a human universality, but it is not something given; it is being perpetually made. I make this universality in choosing myself; I also make it by understanding the purpose of any other man, of whatever epoch. This absoluteness of the act of choice does not alter the relativity of each epoch.

What is at the very heart and centre of existentialism, is the absolute character of the free commitment, by which every man realises himself in realising a type of humanity — a commitment always understandable, to no matter whom in no matter what epoch — and its bearing upon the relativity of the cultural pattern which may result from such absolute commitment. One must observe equally the relativity of Cartesianism and the absolute character of the Cartesian commitment. In this sense you may say, if you like, that every one of us makes the absolute by breathing, by eating, by sleeping or by behaving in any fashion whatsoever. There is no difference between free being—being as self-committal, as existence choosing its essence—and absolute being. And there is no difference whatever between being as an absolute, temporarily localised—that is, localised in history—and universally intelligible being.

This does not completely refute the charge of subjectivism. Indeed that objection appears in several other forms, of which the first is as follows. People say to us, "Then it does not matter what you do," and they say this in various ways. First they tax us with anarchy; then they say, "You cannot judge others, for there is no reason for preferring one purpose to another"; finally, they may say, "Everything being merely voluntary in this choice of yours, you give away with one hand what you pretend to gain with the other." These three are not very serious objections. As to the first, to say that it matters not what you choose is not correct. In one sense choice is possible, but what is not possible is not to choose. I can always choose, but I must know that if I do not choose, that is still a choice. This, although it may appear merely formal, is of great importance as a limit to fantasy and caprice. For, when I confront a real situation—for example, that I am a sexual being, able to have relations with a being of the other sex and able to have children—I am obliged to choose my attitude to it, and in every respect I bear the responsibility of the choice which, in committing myself, also commits the whole of humanity. Even if my choice is determined by no *à priori* value whatever, it can have nothing to do with caprice: and if anyone thinks that this is only Gide's theory of the *acte gratuit* over again, he has failed to see the enormous difference between this theory and that of Gide. Gide does not know what a situation is, his "act" is one of pure caprice. In our view, on the contrary, man finds himself in an organised situation in which he is himself involved: his choice involves mankind in its entirety, and he cannot avoid choosing. Either he must remain single, or he must marry without having children, or he must marry and have children. In any case, and whichever he may choose, it is impossible for him, in respect of this situation, not to take complete responsibility. Doubtless he chooses without reference to any pre-established values, but it is unjust to tax him with caprice. Rather let us say that the moral choice is comparable to the construction of a work of art.

But here I must at once digress to make it quite clear that we are not propounding an aesthetic morality, for our adversaries are disingenuous enough to reproach us even with that. I mention the work of art only by way of comparison. That being understood, does anyone reproach an artist when he paints a picture for not following rules established *à priori*? Does one ever ask what is the picture that he ought to paint? As everyone knows, there is no pre-defined picture for him to make; the artist applies himself to the composition of a picture, and the picture that ought to be made is precisely that which he will have made. As everyone knows, there are no aesthetic values *à priori*, but there are values which will appear in due course in the coherence of the picture, in the relation between the will to create and the finished work. No one can tell what the painting of tomorrow will be like; one cannot judge a painting until it is done. What has that to do with morality? We are in the same creative situation. We never speak of a work of art as irresponsible; when we are discussing a canvas by Picasso, we understand very well that the composition became what it is at the time when he was painting it, and that his works are part and parcel of his entire life.

It is the same upon the plane of morality. There is this in common between art and morality, that in both we have to do with creation and invention. We cannot decide *à priori* what it is that should be done. I think it was made sufficiently clear to you in the case of that student who came to see me, that to whatever ethical system he might appeal, the Kantian or any other, he could find no sort of guidance whatever; he was obliged to invent the law for himself. Certainly we cannot say that this man, in choosing to remain with his mother — that is, in taking sentiment, personal devotion and concrete charity as his moral foundations — would be making an irresponsible choice, nor could we do so if he preferred the sacrifice of going away to England. Man makes himself; he is not found ready-made; he makes himself by the choice of his morality, and he cannot but choose a morality, such is the pressure of circumstances upon him. We define man only in relation to his commitments; it is therefore absurd to reproach us for irresponsibility in our choice.

In the second place, people say to us, "You are unable to judge others." This is true in one sense and false in another. It is true in this sense, that whenever a man chooses his purpose and his commitment in all clearness and in all sincerity, whatever that purpose may be it is impossible to prefer another for him. It is true in the sense that we do not believe in progress. Progress implies amelioration; but man is always the same, being a situation which is always changing, and choice remains always a choice in the situation. The moral problem has not changed since the time when it was a choice between slavery and anti-slavery—from the time of the war of Secession, for example, until the present moment when one chooses between the MRP[4] and the Communists.

We can judge, nevertheless, for, as I have said, one chooses in view of others, and in view of others one chooses himself. One can judge, first—and perhaps this is not a judgement of value, but it is a logical judgement —that in certain cases choice is founded upon an error, and in others upon the truth. One can judge a man by saying that he deceives himself. Since we have defined the situation of man as one of free choice, without excuse and without help, any man who takes refuge behind the excuse of his passions, or by inventing some deterministic doctrine, is a self-deceiver. One may object: "But why

---

4 Mouvement Républicain Populaire.

should he not choose to deceive himself?" I reply that it is not for me to judge him morally, but I define his self-deception as an error. Here one cannot avoid pronouncing a judgement of truth. The self-deception is evidently a falsehood, because it is a dissimulation of man's complete liberty of commitment. Upon this same level, I say that it is also a self-deception if I choose to declare that certain values are incumbent upon me; I am in contradiction with myself if I will these values and at the same time say that they impose themselves upon me. If anyone says to me, "And what if I wish to deceive myself?" I answer, "There is no reason why you should not, but I declare that you are doing so, and that the attitude of strict consistency alone is that of good faith." Furthermore, I can pronounce a moral judgement. For I declare that freedom, in respect of concrete circumstances, can have no other end and aim but itself; and when once a man has seen that values depend upon himself, in that state of forsakenness he can will only one thing, and that is freedom as the foundation of all values. That does not mean that he wills it in the abstract: it simply means that the actions of men of good faith have, as their ultimate significance, the quest of freedom itself as such. A man who belongs to some communist or revolutionary society wills certain concrete ends, which imply the will to freedom, but that freedom is willed in community. We will freedom for freedom's sake, and in and through particular circumstances. And in thus willing freedom, we discover that it depends entirely upon the freedom of others and that the freedom of others depends upon our own. Obviously, freedom as the definition of a man does not depend upon others, but as soon as there is a commitment, I am obliged to will the liberty of others at the same time as mine. I cannot make liberty my aim unless I make that of others equally my aim. Consequently, when I recognise, as entirely authentic, that man is a being whose existence precedes his essence, and that he is a free being who cannot, in any circumstances, but will his freedom, at the same time I realise that I cannot not will the freedom of others. Thus, in the name of that will to freedom which is implied in freedom itself, I can form judgements upon those who seek to hide from themselves the wholly voluntary nature of their existence and its complete freedom. Those who hide from this total freedom, in a guise of solemnity or with deterministic excuses, I shall call cowards. Others, who try to show that their existence is necessary, when it is merely an accident of the appearance of the human race on earth,—I shall call scum. But neither cowards nor scum can be identified except upon the plane of strict authenticity. Thus, although the content of morality is variable, a certain form of this morality is universal. Kant declared that freedom is a will both to itself and to the freedom of others. Agreed: but he thinks that the formal and the universal suffice for the constitution of a morality. We think, on the contrary, that principles that are too abstract break down when we come to defining action. To take once again the case of that student; by what authority, in the name of what golden rule of morality, do you think he could have decided, in perfect peace of mind, either to abandon his mother or to remain with her? There are no means of judging. The content is always concrete, and therefore unpredictable; it has always to be invented. The one thing that counts, is to know whether the invention is made in the name of freedom.

Let us, for example, examine the two following cases, and you will see how far they are similar in spite of their difference. Let us take *The Mill on the Floss*. We find here a certain young woman, Maggie Tulliver, who is an incarnation of the value of passion and is aware of it. She is in love with a young man, Stephen, who is engaged to another, an insignificant young woman. This

Jean-Paul Sartre

Maggie Tulliver, instead of heedlessly seeking her own happiness, chooses in the name of human solidarity to sacrifice herself and to give up the man she loves. On the other hand, La Sanseverina in Stendhal's *Chartreuse de Parme*, believing that it is passion which endows man with his real value, would have declared that a grand passion justifies its sacrifices, and must be preferred to the banality of such conjugal love as would unite Stephen to the little goose he was engaged to marry. It is the latter that she would have chosen to sacrifice in realising her own happiness, and, as Stendhal shows, she would also sacrifice herself upon the plane of passion if life made that demand upon her. Here we are facing two clearly opposed moralities; but I claim that they are equivalent, seeing that in both cases the overruling aim is freedom. You can imagine two attitudes exactly similar in effect, in that one girl might prefer, in resignation, to give up her lover whilst the other preferred, in fulfilment of sexual desire, to ignore the prior engagement of the man she loved; and, externally, these two cases might appear the same as the two we have just cited, while being in fact entirely different. The attitude of La Sanseverina is much nearer to that of Maggie Tulliver than to one of careless greed. Thus, you see, the second objection is at once true and false. One can choose anything, but only if it is upon the plane of free commitment.

The third objection, stated by saying, "You take with one hand what you give with the other," means, at bottom, "your values are not serious, since you choose them yourselves." To that I can only say that I am very sorry that it should be so; but if I have excluded God the Father, there must be somebody to invent values. We have to take things as they are. And moreover, to say that we invent values means neither more nor less than this; that there is no sense in life *à priori*. Life is nothing until it is lived; but it is yours to make sense of, and the value of it is nothing else but the sense that you choose. Therefore, you can see that there is a possibility of creating a human community. I have been reproached for suggesting that existentialism is a form of humanism: people have said to me, "But you have written in your *Nauseé* that the humanists are wrong, you have even ridiculed a certain type of humanism, why do you now go back upon that?" In reality, the word humanism has two very different meanings. One may understand by humanism a theory which upholds man as the end-in-itself and as the supreme value. Humanism in this sense appears, for instance, in Cocteau's story *Round the World in 80 Days*,

Jean-Paul Sartre

in which one of the characters declares, because he is flying over mountains in an aeroplane, "Man is magnificent!" This signifies that although I, personally, have not built aeroplanes I have the benefit of those particular inventions and that I personally, being a man, can consider myself responsible for, and honoured by, achievements that are peculiar to some men. It is to assume that we can ascribe value to man according to the most distinguished deeds of certain men. That kind of humanism is absurd, for only the dog or the horse would be in a position to pronounce a general judgement upon man and declare that he is magnificent, which they have never been such fools as to do — at least, not as far as I know. But neither is it admissible that a man should pronounce judgement upon Man. Existentialism dispenses with any judgement of this sort: an existentialist will never take man as the end, since man is still to be determined. And we have no right to believe that humanity is something to which we could set up a cult, after the manner of Auguste Comte. The cult of humanity ends in Comtian humanism, shut-in upon itself, and — this must be said — in Fascism. We do not want a humanism like that.

But there is another sense of the word, of which the fundamental meaning is this: Man is all the time outside of himself: it is in projecting and losing himself beyond himself that he makes man to exist; and, on the other hand, it is by pursuing transcendent aims that he himself is able to exist. Since man is thus self-surpassing, and can grasp objects only in relation to his self-surpassing, he is himself the heart and centre of his transcendence. There is no other universe except the human universe, the universe of human subjectivity. This relation of transcendence as constitutive of man (not in the sense that God is transcendent, but in the sense of self-surpassing) with subjectivity (in such a sense that man is not shut up in himself but forever present in a human universe) — it is this that we call existential humanism. This is humanism, because we remind man that there is no legislator but himself; that he himself, thus abandoned, must decide for himself; also because we show that it is not by turning back upon himself, but always by seeking, beyond himself, an aim which is one of liberation or of some particular realisation, that man can realise himself as truly human.

You can see from these few reflections that nothing could be more unjust than the objections people raise against us. Existentialism is nothing else but an attempt to draw the full conclusions from a consistently atheistic position. Its intention is not in the least that of plunging men into despair. And if by despair one means—as the Christians do—any attitude of unbelief, the despair of the existentialists is something different. Existentialism is not atheist in the sense that it would exhaust itself in demonstrations of the non-existence of God. It declares, rather, that even if God existed that would make no difference from its point of view. Not that we believe God does exist, but we think that the real problem is not that of His existence; what man needs is to find himself again and to understand that nothing can save him from himself, not even a valid proof of the existence of God. In this sense existentialism is optimistic, it is a doctrine of action, and it is only by self-deception, by confusing their own despair with ours that Christians can describe us as without hope.

Discussion

Questioner
I do not know whether this attempt to make yourself understood will make you better understood, or less so; but I think that the explanation in *Action* will only make people misunderstand you more. The words "despair" and "abandonment" have a much wider resonance in an existential context. And it seems to me that despair or anguish means, to you, something more fundamental than the responsibility of the man who feels he is alone and has to make decisions. It is a state of consciousness of the human predicament which does not arise all the time. That one is choosing whom one is to be, is admitted, but anguish and despair do not appear concurrently.

M. Sartre
Obviously I do not mean that whenever I choose between a millefeuille and a chocolate éclair, I choose in anguish.

Discussion

Anguish is constant in this sense—that my original choice is something constant. Indeed, this anguish is, in my view, the complete absence of justification at the same time as one is responsible in regard to everyone.

Questioner
I was alluding to the point of view of the explanation published in *Action*, in which it seemed to me that your own point of view was somewhat weakened.

M. Sartre
Frankly it is possible that my themes have been rather weakened in *Action*. It often happens that people who come and put questions to me are not qualified to do so. I am then presented with two alternatives, that of refusing to answer or that of accepting discussion upon the level of popularisation. I have chosen the latter because, after all, when one expounds theories in a class of philosophy one consents to some weakening of an idea in order to make it understood, and it is not such a bad thing to do. If one has a theory of commitment one must commit oneself to see it through. If in truth existential philosophy is above all a philosophy which says that existence precedes essence, it must be lived to be really sincere; and to live as

an existentialist is to consent to pay for this teaching, not to put it into books. If you want this philosophy to be indeed a commitment, you have to render some account of it to people who discuss it upon the political or the moral plane.

You reproach me for using the word "humanism." I do so because that is how the problem presents itself. One must either keep the doctrine strictly to the philosophic plane and rely upon chance for any action upon it, or else, seeing that people demand something else, and since its intention is to be a commitment, one must consent to its popularisation — provided one does not thereby distort it.

Questioner

Those who want to understand you will understand, and those who do not want to will not understand you.

M. Sartre

You seem to conceive the part played by philosophy in this civilisation in a sense that has been outmoded by events. Until recently philosophers were attacked only by other philosophers. The public understood nothing of it and cared less. Now, however, they have made

Discussion

philosophy come right down into the marketplace. Marx himself never ceased to popularise his thought. The manifesto is the popularisation of an idea.

Questioner
The original choice of Marx was a revolutionary one.

M. Sartre
He must be a cunning fellow indeed who can say whether Marx chose himself first as a revolutionary and then as a philosopher, or first as a philosopher and as a revolutionary afterwards. He is both a philosopher and a revolutionary — that is a whole. To say that he chose himself first as a revolutionary — what does that mean?

Questioner
The *Communist Manifesto* does not look to me like a popularisation; it is a weapon of war. I cannot believe that it was not an act of commitment.

As soon as Marx concluded that the revolution was necessary, his first action was his *Communist Manifesto*, which was a political action. The *Communist Manifesto* is the bond between the philosophy of Marx and Communism. Whatever may be the morality you hold, one can feel no such close logical connection between that morality and your philosophy as there is between the Communist Manifesto and Marx's philosophy.

M. Sartre

We are dealing with a morality of freedom. So long as there is no contradiction between that morality and our philosophy, nothing more is required. Types of commitment differ from one epoch to another. In one epoch, in which to commit oneself was to make revolution, one had to write the *Manifesto*. In such an epoch as ours, in which there are various parties, each advertising itself as the revolution, commitment does not consist in joining one of them, but in seeking to clarify the conception, in order to define the situation and at the same time to try to influence the different revolutionary parties.

M. Naville

The question one must ask oneself, arising from the point of view that you have just indicated, is this: Will not your doctrine present itself, in the period now beginning, as the resurrection of radical-socialism? This may seem fantastic, but it is the way in which one must now frame the question. You place yourself, by the way, at all sorts

Discussion

of points of view; but if one looks for the actual point of convergence, to which all these points of view and aspects of existential thought are tending, I have the impression that it turns out to be a kind of resurrection of liberalism. Your philosophy seeks to revive, in the quite peculiar conditions which are our present historical conditions, what is essential in radical-socialism, in liberal humanism. What gives it its distinctive character, is the fact that the social crisis of the world has gone too far for the old liberalism, it puts liberalism to torture, to anguish. I believe that one could find several rather profound reasons for this evaluation, even if one kept within your own terms. It follows from the present exposition, that existentialism presents itself as a form of humanism and of a philosophy of freedom, which is at bottom a precommitment, and that is a purpose undefined. You put in the forefront, as do many others, the dignity of man, the eminent value of personality. These are themes which, all things considered, are not so far from those of the old liberalism. To justify them, you make distinction between two meanings of "the condition of man" and between two meanings of several terms which are in common use. The significance of these terms has, however, a whole history, and their equivocal character is not the result of chance.

Existentialism and Humanism

To rescue them, you would invent new meanings for them. I will pass over all the special questions of philosophic technique which this raises, interesting and important as they are; and, confining myself to the terms that I have just heard, I will fasten upon the fundamental point which shows that, in spite of your distinction between two meanings of humanism, the meaning that you hold is, after all, the old one.

Man presents himself as a choice to be made. Very well. He is, first and foremost, his existence at the present instant, and he stands outside of natural determinism. He is not defined by anything prior to himself, but by his present functioning as an individual. There is no human nature superior to him, but a specific existence is given to him at a given moment. I ask myself whether "existence" taken in this sense is not another form of the concept of human nature which, for historical reasons, is appearing in a novel guise. Is it not very similar—more so than it looks at first sight—to human nature as it was defined in the eighteenth century, the conception which you say you repudiate? For this reappears in and very largely underlies the expression "the condition of man" as it is used in existentialism. Your conception of the human condition is a substitute for human nature,

Discussion

just as you substitute lived experience for common experience or scientific experiment.

If we consider human conditions as conditions defined by X, which is the X of the subject, and not by the natural environment, not by positive determinants, one is considering human nature under another form. It is a nature-condition, if you like, which is not to say that it is definable simply as an abstract type of nature; it is revealed in ways much more difficult to formulate for reasons which, in my view, are historical. In these days, human nature is expressing itself in a social framework that is undergoing a general disintegration of social orders and social classes, in conflicts that cut across them, and in a stirring-together of all races and nations. The notion of a uniform and schematic human nature cannot now be presented with the same character of generality nor take on the same aspect of universality as in the eighteenth century, an epoch when it appeared to be definable upon a basis of continuous progress. In these days we are concerned with an expression of human nature which both thoughtful and simple people call the condition of man. Their presentation of this is vague, chaotic and generally of an aspect that is, so to speak, dramatic; imposed by the circumstances. And, in so far as they do not want

Existentialism and Humanism

to go beyond the general expression of that condition into a deterministic enquiry unto what the effective conditions are, they maintain the type and the scheme of an abstract expression, analogous to that of human nature.

This existentialism does depend upon a notion of the nature of man, but this time it is not a nature that has pride in itself, but one that is fearful, uncertain and forlorn. And, indeed, when the existentialist speaks of the condition of man, he is speaking of a condition in which he is not yet really committed to what existentialism calls purposes—and which is, consequently, a pre-condition. We have here a pre-engagement, not a commitment, not even a real condition. It is not by accident, then, that this "condition of man" is defined primarily by its general, humanist character. In the past, when one spoke of human nature, one was thinking of something more limited than if one were speaking of a condition in general. For nature—that is already something else: in a sense it is something more than a condition. Human nature is not a modality in the sense that the condition of man is a modality. For that reason it would be better, in my view, to speak of naturalism than of humanism. In naturalism there is an implication of realities more general than are implied in humanism—at least, in the

Discussion

---

sense in which you take the term "humanism"—we are dealing with reality itself. As to human nature, the discussion of it needs to be widened: for the historical point of view must also be considered. The primary reality is that of nature, of which human reality is only one function. But for that, one must admit the truth of history, and the existentialist will not, as a rule, admit the truth of human history any more than that of natural history in general. Nevertheless, it is history which makes individuals: it is because of their actual history, from the moment when they are conceived, that they are neither born nor do they live in a world which provides an abstract condition for them. Because of their history they appear in a world of which they themselves have always been part and parcel, by which they are conditioned and to the conditions of which they contribute, even as the mother conditions her child and the child also conditions her from the beginning of its gestation. It is only from this point of view that we have any right to speak of the condition of man as of a primary reality. One ought rather to say that the primary reality is a natural condition and not a human condition. These are merely current and common opinions that I am repeating, but in no way whatever that I can see does the existential argument refute them. After all, if it is certain that there is no human nature in the abstract, no essence of man apart from or anterior to his existence, it is also certain that there is no human condition in general—not even if you mean by condition a certain set of concrete circumstances or situations, for in your view these are not articulated. In any case, upon this subject Marxism has a different idea, that of nature within man and man within nature, which is not necessarily defined from an individual point of view.

This means that there are laws of the functioning of man, as of every other object of science, which constitute, in the full sense of the word, his nature. That nature is variable, it is true, but bears little resemblance to a phenomenology—that is, to any perception of it that is felt, empirical, or lived, or such as is given by common sense or rather by the assumed common sense of the philosophers. Thus understood, the conception of human nature as the men of the eighteenth century had it, was undoubtedly much nearer to that of Marx than is its existential substitute, "the condition of man"—which is a pure phenomenology of his situation.

In these days, unfortunately, humanism is a word employed to identify philosophic tendencies, not only in two senses but in three, four, five, or six. We are all humanists today, even certain Marxists. Those who reveal themselves as classical rationalists are humanists in a sense that has gone sour on us, derived from the liberal ideas of the last century, a liberalism refracted throughout the contemporary crisis. If Marxists can claim to be humanists, the various religions, Christian, Hindu and many others, also claim above all that they are humanist; so do the existentialists in their turn and, in a general way, all the philosophies. Actually, many political movements protest no less that they are humanist. What all this amounts to is a kind of attempt to reinstate a philosophy which, for all its claims, refuses in the last resort to commit itself, not only from the political or social standpoint, but also in the deeper philosophic sense. When Christianity claims to be humanist before all else, it is because it refuses to commit itself, because it cannot— that is, it cannot side with the progressive forces in the conflict, because it is holding on to reactionary positions in face of the revolution. When the pseudo-Marxists or the liberals place the rights of the personality above everything, it is because they recoil before the exigencies of the present world situation. Just so the existentialist, like the liberal, puts in a claim for man in general because he cannot manage to formulate such a position as the events require, and the only progressive position that is known is that of Marxism. Marxism alone states the real problems of the age.

It is not true that a man has freedom of choice, in the sense that by that choice he confers upon his activity a meaning it would not otherwise have. It is not enough to say that men can strive for freedom without knowing that they strive for it—or, if we give the fullest meaning to that recognition, it means that men can engage in the struggle for a cause which overrules them, which is to say that they can act within a frame greater than themselves, and not merely act out of themselves. For in the end, if a man strives for freedom without knowing it, without being able to say precisely how or to what end he is striving, what does that signify? That his actions are going to bring about a succession of consequences weaving themselves into a whole network of causality of which he cannot grasp all the effects, but which, all the same, round off his action and endow it with a meaning, in function with the activity of others—and not only that of other men, but of the natural environment in which those men act. But, from your point of view, the choice is a pre-choice—I come back again to that prefix, for I

Discussion

think you still interpose a reserve. In this kind of pre-choice one is concerned with the freedom of a prior indifference. But your conception of the condition and the freedom of man is linked to a certain definition of the objective upon which I have a word to say: it is, indeed, upon this idea of the world of objects as utilities that you base everything else. From an image of beings existing in discontinuity, you form a picture of a discontinuous world of objects, in which there is no causality, excepting that strange variety of causal relatedness which is that of utility—passive, incomprehensible and contemptible. Existential man stumbles about in a world of implements, of untidy obstacles, entangled and piled up one upon another in a fantastic desire to make them serve one another, but all branded with the stigma, so frightful in the eyes of idealists, of their so-called pure exteriority. This implemental mode of determinism is, however, a-causal. For where is the beginning or the end of such a world, the definition of which, moreover, is wholly arbitrary and in no way agrees with the data of modern science? For us it neither begins nor ends anywhere, for the separation which the existentialist inflicts upon it—separation from nature, or rather from the condition of man—makes it unreal. There is one world and only one, in our view, and the whole of this world—both men and things, if you must make that distinction—may be seen, in certain variable conditions, under the sign of objectivity. The utility of stars, of anger, of a flower? I will not argue about such things: but I maintain that your freedom, your idealism, is made out of an arbitrary contempt for things. And yet things are very different from the description that you give of them. You admit their existence in their own right, and so far so good. But it is a purely privative existence, one of permanent hostility. The physical and biological universe is never, in your eyes, a condition or a source of conditioning—that word, in its full and practical sense, has no more meaning for you than has the word "cause." That is why the objective universe is, for existential man, nothing but an occasion of vexation, a thing elusive, fundamentally indifferent, a continual mere probability—in short, the very opposite of what it is to the Marxist materialist.

For all these reasons and for some others, you can only conceive the commitment of philosophy as an arbitrary decision which you describe as free. You denature history, even that of Marx, when you say that he has outlined a philosophy because he was committed to it. On

Discussion

the contrary; the commitment, or rather the social and political action, was a determinant of his thinking in a more general sense. It was out of a multiplicity of experiences that he distilled his doctrines. It appears evident to me that the development of philosophic thinking in Marx took place in conscious connection with the development of politics and society. That is more or less the case, moreover, with all previous philosophers. Kant is a systematic philosopher who is known to have refrained from all political activity, but that does not mean that his philosophy did not play a certain political rôle — Kant, the German Robespierre, as Heine called him. And, even to the extent that one might admit, of the epoch of Descartes for example, that the development of philosophy played no direct part in politics — which is however erroneous — it has become impossible to say so since the last century. In these days to seek to re-establish, in any form whatsoever, a position anterior to Marxism — I call that going back to radical-socialism.

In so far as existentialism is engendering a will to revolution it ought, therefore, to undertake first of all a work of self-criticism. I do not think it will do this very cheerfully, but it must be done. It will have to undergo a crisis in the persons of those who advocate it — a dialectical crisis—if it is still to retain, in some sense, certain positions not devoid of value which are held by some of its partisans. That seems to me all the more necessary because I have noted that some of them have been arguing from existentialism to social conclusions that are most disquieting, indeed obviously retrograde. One of them wrote, at the end of an analysis, that phenomenology could perform a special social service today, by providing the *petite*-bourgeoisie with a philosophy which would enable them to live and to become the vanguard of the international revolutionary movement. By this interpretation of conscientious intentions, one could give the *petite*-bourgeoisie a philosophy corresponding to its existence, and it could become the advance guard of the world revolutionary movement! I mention this as an example, and I could give you others of the same kind, showing that a certain number of persons, who are moreover deeply committed, and find themselves much drawn to the existential theme, are beginning to elaborate it into political theories. But after all, and here I come back to what I said at the beginning, these are theories coloured with neo-liberalism, with neo-radical-socialism. That is certainly a danger. What chiefly interests us is not any research into the dialectical coherence between all the

Discussion

different grounds touched upon by existentialism, but to see the orientation of these themes. For little by little, perhaps unknown to their defenders, and undertaken as an enquiry, a theory, as an attitude, they do lead to something. Not, of course, to quietism; to talk of quietism in the present epoch would be a losing game indeed, in fact an impossible one: but to something very like "attentism."[5] That may perhaps be not inconsistent with certain kinds of individual commitment; but it is inconsistent with any search for a commitment of collective value—especially of a prescriptive value. Why should existentialism not give any directions? In the name of freedom? But if this philosophy tends in the direction indicated by Sartre, it ought to give directives. It ought, in 1945, to tell us whether to join the UDSR.[6] or the Socialist Party, the Communist Party or another: it ought to say whether it is on the side of the workers or on that of the *petite*-bourgeoisie.

---

5 The attentistes, as they were called, were those who neither collaborated with the German occupation nor resisted it: but waited (as they said) for the time when the Allies would invade and make resistance more efficacious, or—as their enemies said—waited to join the winning side.

6 Union Des Socialistes Republicains.

M. Sartre

It is rather difficult to give you a complete answer. You have said so many things. But I will try to reply to a few points that I have noted down. First, I must say that you take up a dogmatic position. You say that we take up a position anterior to Marxism, that we are advancing towards the rear. I consider that what you have to prove is that the position we are seeking to establish is not post-Marxian. As to that I will not argue, but I would like to ask you how you come by your conception of "the truth." You think there are some things that are absolutely true, for you present your objections in the name of a certitude. But if all men are objects as you say, whence have you such a certitude. You say it is in the name of human dignity that man refuses to regard man as an object. That is false: it is for a reason of a philosophic and logical order: if you postulate a universe of objects, truth disappears. The objective world is the world of the probable. You ought to recognise that every theory, whether scientific or philosophic, is one of probability. The proof of this is that scientific and historical theses vary, and that they are made in the form of hypotheses. If we admit that the objective world, the world of the probable, is one, we have still no more than a world of probabilities; and in

Discussion

that case since the probability depends upon our having acquired some truths, whence comes the certitude? Our subjectivism allows us some certitudes, and we are thus enabled to rejoin you upon the plane of the probable. We can thus justify the dogmatism which you have demonstrated throughout your discourse, though it is incomprehensible from the position that you take. If you do not define the truth, how can you conceive the theory of Marx otherwise than as a doctrine which appears, disappears, is modified and has no more than theoretical value? How can one make a dialectic of history unless one begins by postulating a certain number of rules? We deduce these from the Cartesian *cogito*: we can only find them by placing ourselves firmly upon the ground of subjectivity. We have never disputed the fact that, continually, man is an object to man. But reciprocally, in order to grasp the object as it is, there must be a subject which attains to itself as subject.

Then, you speak of a condition of man, which you sometimes call a pre-condition, and you speak of pre-determination. What has escaped your notice here, is that we adhere to much that is in the Marxian descriptions. You cannot criticise me as you would criticise the men of the eighteenth century, who were ignorant of the whole question. We have known for a long time all that you have been telling us about determinism. For us the real problem is to define conditions in which there can be universality. Since there is no human nature, how can one preserve, throughout the continual changes of history, universal principles sufficient to interpret, for instance, the phenomenon of Spartacus, which presupposes a minimum understanding of that epoch? We are in agreement upon this point—that there is no human nature; in other words, each epoch develops according to dialectical laws, and men depend upon their epoch and not upon human nature.

M. Naville

When you seek to interpret, you say: "This is so because we are dealing with a particular situation." For our part, we consider what is analogous or different in the social life of that epoch compared with that of our own. If on the other hand, we tried to analyse the analogy itself as a function of some abstract kind, we should never arrive at anything. If you suppose that, after two thousand years, one has no means of analysing the present situation except certain observations upon the condition of man in general, how could one conduct an analysis that was retrospective? One could not do it.

Discussion

M. Sartre

We have never doubted the need for analysis either of human conditions or of individual intentions. That which we call the situation is, precisely, the whole of the conditions, not only material but psycho-analytic, which, in the epoch under consideration, define it precisely as a whole.

M. Naville

I do not believe that your definition is in conformity with your texts. Anyhow, it clearly appears that your conception of the situation is in no way identifiable, even remotely, with any Marxist conception, in that it denies causality. Your definition is not precise: it often slips cleverly from one position to another, without defining either in a sufficiently rigorous manner. For us, a situation is a totality that is constructed, and that reveals itself, by a whole series of determining factors, and these determinants are causal, including causality of a statistical kind.

M. Sartre

You talk to me about causality of a statistical order. That is meaningless. Will you tell me, precisely and clearly, what you understand by causality? I will believe in the Marxian causality upon the very day when a Marxian explains it to me. Whenever anyone speaks to you of freedom you spend your time in saying, "Excuse me, but there is causality." But of this secret causality, which has no meaning except in Hegel, you can render no account. You have a dream about the Marxian causality.

M. Naville
Do you admit the existence of scientific truth? There may be spheres in which no kind of truth is predicable. But the world of objects—this you will nevertheless admit, I hope—is the world with which the sciences are concerned. Yet for you, this is a world in which there are only probabilities, never amounting to the truth. The world of objects, then, which is that of science, admits of no absolute truth. But it does attain to relative truth. Now, you will admit that the sciences employ the notion of causality?

M. Sartre
Certainly not. The sciences are abstract; they study the variations of factors that are equally abstract, and not real causality. We are concerned with universal factors

Discussion

upon a plane where their relations can always be studied: whereas, in Marxism, one is engaged in the study of a single totality, in which one searches for causality. But it is not at all the same thing as scientific causality.

M. Naville
You gave an example, and developed it at length — that of a young man who came to consult you.

M. Sartre
Was it not a question of freedom?

M. Naville
He ought to have been answered. I would have endeavoured to ascertain what were his capabilities, his age, his financial resources; and to look into his relation to his mother. Perhaps I should have pronounced a merely probable opinion, but I would most certainly have tried to arrive at a definite point of view, though it might have been proved wrong when acted upon. Most certainly I would have urged him to do something.

M. Sartre

If he comes to ask your advice, it is because he has already chosen the answer. Practically, I should have been very well able to give him some advice. But as he was seeking freedom I wanted to let him decide. Besides, I knew what he was going to do, and that is what he did.